Jarlath Regan (born 1980) is a stand-up comedian, actor, writer and cartoonist. He grew up in The Curragh of Kildare, doodling, cycling to school across the windswept plains and dreaming of playing NBA basketball. As a comedian he has performed at every major comedy festival across the world, including the Edinburgh Fringe, Montreal Just for Laughs and Melbourne Comedy Festival. He has made several television appearances including *The Panel* (RTÉ), *Nobody Knows Jarlath Regan* (TV3) and *The World Stands Up* (Comedy Central).

Jarlath started making twisted greetings cards in 2006 when his friend Cormac O'Connor helped him to bring his drawings to the world through Jigser Cards. He sells his cards from his website, **www.jigser.com**, and packages and sends them himself. Currently living in Dublin, he prefers to commute to most of his gigs by bicycle.

How to Break Bad News

Greetings from the Dark Side

Jarlath Regan

TRANSWORLD IRELAND

TRANSWORLD IRELAND
an imprint of The Random House Group Limited
20 Vauxhall Bridge Road, London SW1V 2SA
www.rbooks.co.uk

First published in 2009 by Transworld Ireland,
a division of Transworld Publishers Ltd

A CIP catalogue record for this book
is available from the British Library.

ISBN 9781848270657

Addresses for Random House Group Ltd companies outside the UK
can be found at: www.randomhouse.co.uk
The Random House Group Ltd Reg. No. 954009

The Random House Group Limited supports The Forest Stewardship
Council (FSC), the leading international forest-certification organization. All our
titles that are printed on Greenpeace-approved FSC-certified paper carry the FSC logo.
Our paper procurement policy can be found at
www.rbooks.co.uk/environment

Typeset in jd handcrafted
Printed and bound in Great Britain by
Clays Ltd, St Ives plc

2 4 6 8 10 9 7 5 3 1

For Tina Rowland

Introduction

Throughout my life, I've embarrassed myself in public more than most. Not only have I been caught with my pants down, I've had my pants pulled down and I've split my pants. I've eaten my first pistachio nut with the shell still on, talked about people while they were within earshot, told lies to sound more intelligent, told more lies to prove that I was not lying in the first place (only to be found out within seconds), spilled food down my shirt at black-tie events, forgotten people's names after long conversations, made jokes about car crashes to people I didn't realize had just recovered from car crash injuries, done impersonations of people I thought wouldn't take offence, fallen on my face and pretended not to be hurt, and arranged secret visits to the doctor for treatment of injuries too embarrassing for an eleven-year-old boy to tell his mother about.

Since becoming a stand-up comedian, I've been ridiculed and humiliated on stage in front of hundreds of people. And all my life, I have been blessed with a mind that involuntarily dredges up these memories for me to relive while going about my daily business. There I am, doing the dishes, and suddenly I find myself shuddering as a previously forgotten humiliation comes flooding back in rich Technicolor.

Maybe that's why tales of humiliation make me so happy.

I like hearing stories that make me cringe, because they make me feel normal. They make me happy I wasn't there, happy it wasn't me and happy I'm not the only one who makes social gaffes that people will remember for years to come. That's where the idea for this book came from. If any of the greetings cards in this collection were used with a straight face they could produce moments of embarrassment from which there would be no recovery. Even I, with my obvious talent for self-humiliation, wouldn't be foolish enough to give one of them with a straight face.

The cards you'll find in the following pages are not intended for people who want to break up with their partners, fire their employees, insult others or confess to being racist. These cards are for true friends. For the past six years I have personally written, illustrated and sent these cards to my friends and family to say, 'I'm happy that I know you well enough to know that you will get this joke.'

Jarlath

Acknowledgements

I would like to thank my good friend Cormac O'Connor for the amount of hard work, imagination, talent and good humour he contributed to making this book possible. Without his initiative these drawings might have remained a private joke for my friends and me. Thanks to Ardal for his kind words. Thanks to Faith at Lisa Richards for taking my half-cooked idea to the best people, Eoin and Lauren at Transworld Ireland. I can't imagine two people who could have been more supportive throughout the process of completing this book. Special thanks to Lauren for always believing it was funny, prodding me to get on with it, not telling me to 'shhh' when I got carried away with the excitement of having my own book and for doing an immense amount of work that I will never fully know about.

Thanks to my parents for letting me be whoever I wanted to be. When I was a kid all I wanted to be was the centre of attention. Thanks to my brother and sisters (Adrian, Caragh and Maeve) – you held me down when I got hyper and let me off when I was being adorable. Thanks to Maeve in particular. You are the best friend anyone could ask for.

In no way does the word 'thanks' cover what I owe to Tina Rowland. This is for you, Tina. It simply could not have happened without you. I love you more than you'll ever know.

How to Break Bad News...

Your iPhone may be
cooler than mine...

But my life has
more depth.

I've missed you so much...

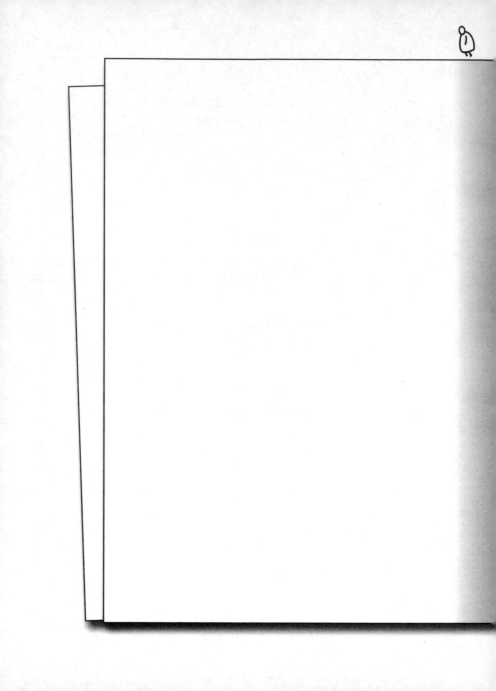

...that I'm now with
someone else.

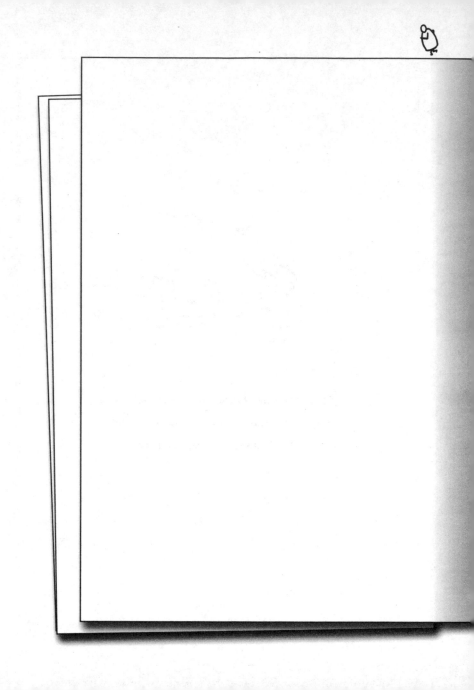

Well now you can,
because you're fired.

Honesty is the best policy...

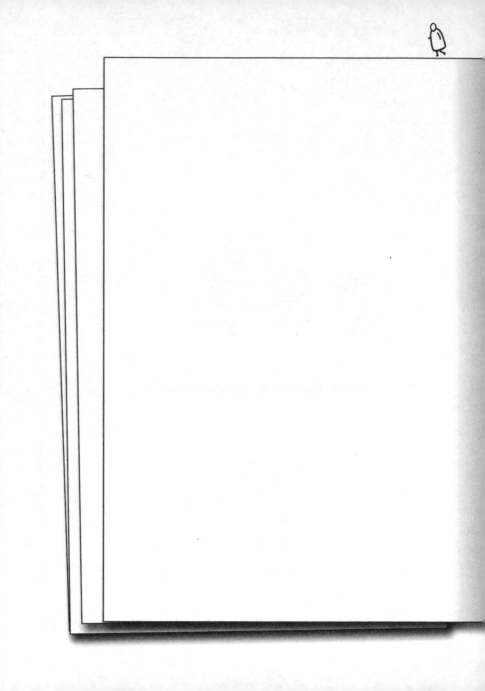

Except in hostage situations.

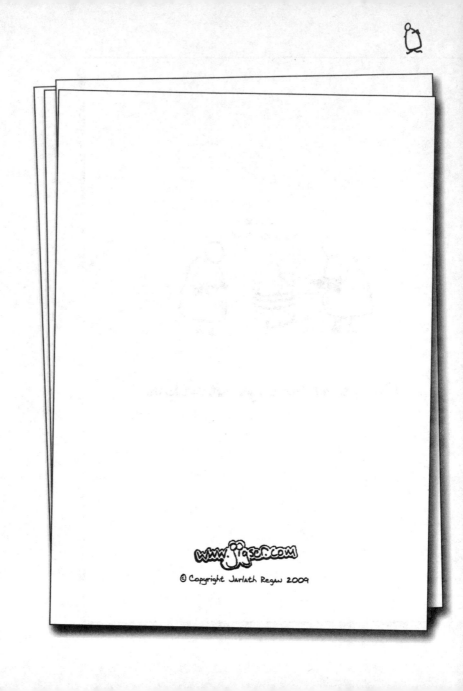

www.jigscom.com

I know I haven't been pulling
my weight around the house or
paying my share of the bills...

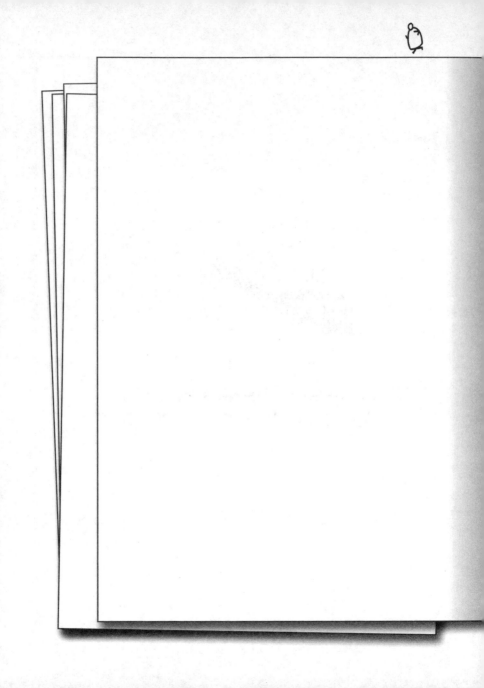

That's because I moved out.

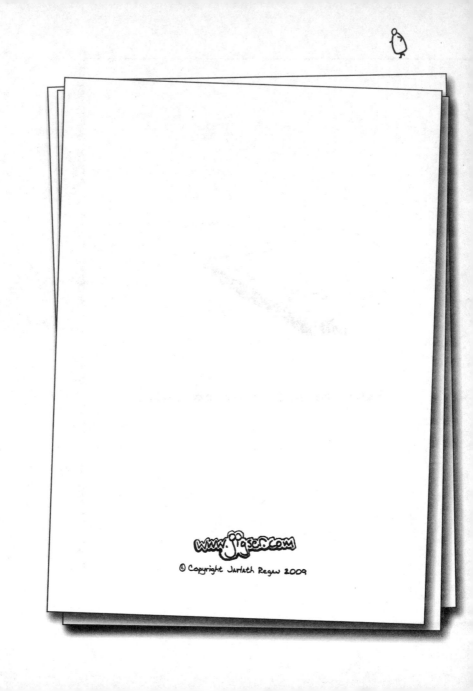

Peter liked to tell Santa his
favourite Christmas cracker
jokes. And although Santa's
laughter was fake...

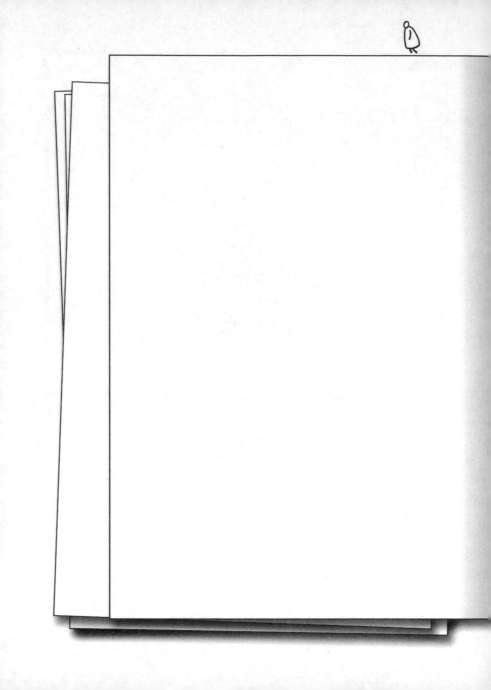

...his hatred of children
was very real.

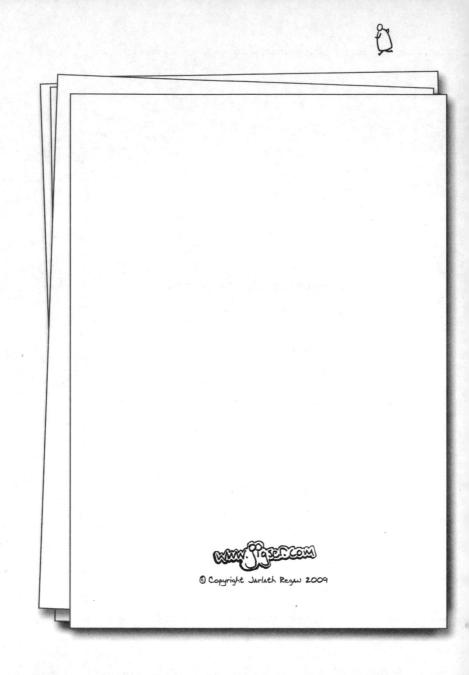

You're the best dad ever!

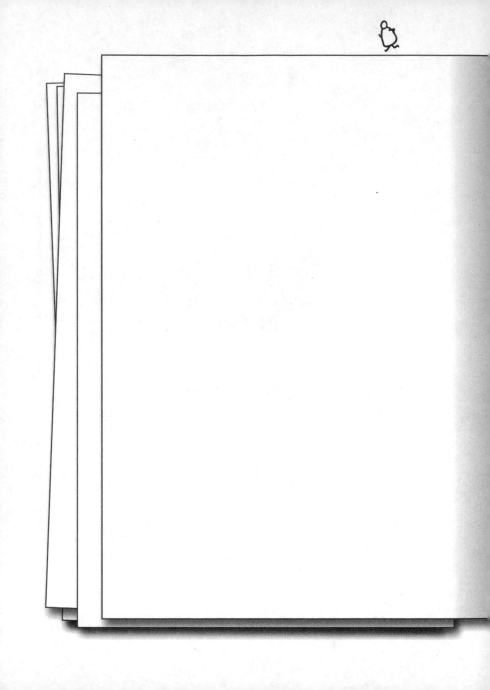

But what would I know,
I grew up in a basement.

This time of year always
reminds me of you...

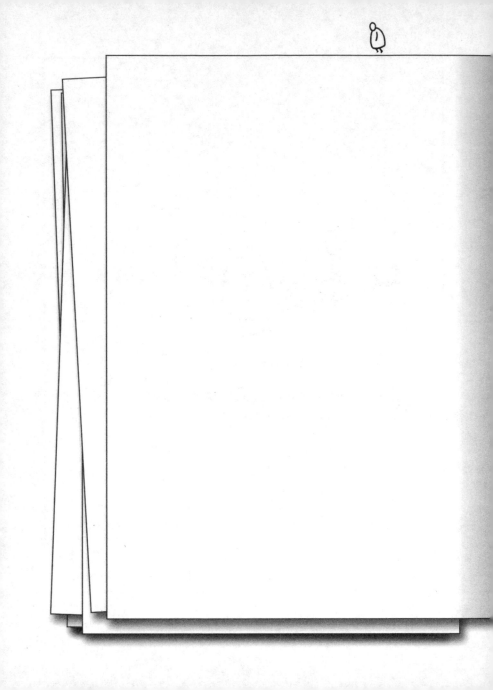

Happy Hallowe'en, you witch.

www.jigser.com

© Copyright Jarlath Regan 2009

Start your day with a
nice cup of coffee...

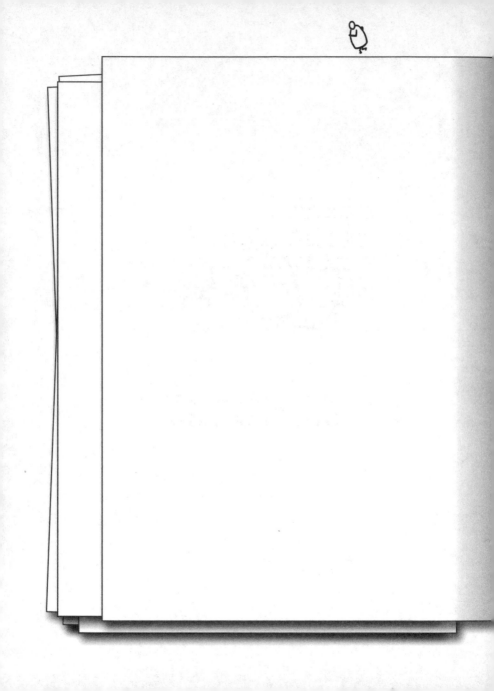

...rather than heroin.

When I said you could
wake me up with oral sex...

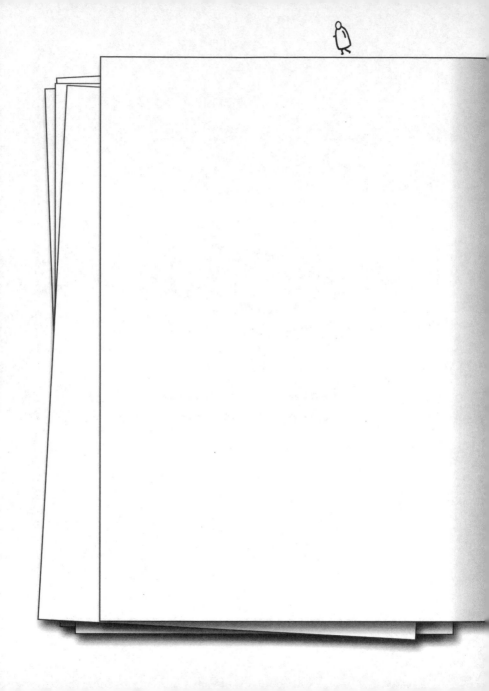

...that's not what I meant.

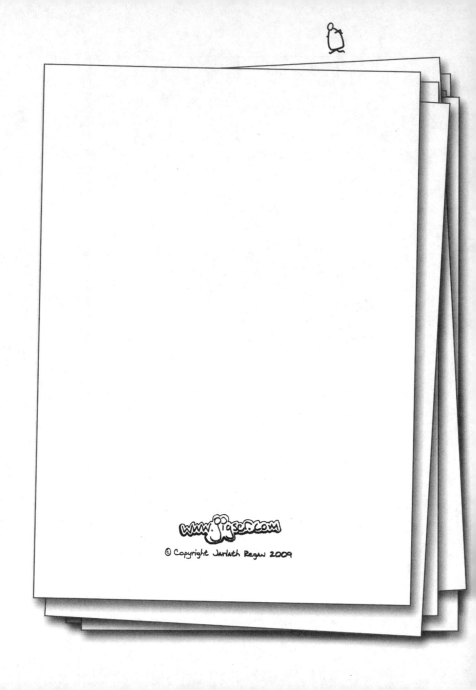

What's the biggest
miracle of Christmas?

Me not killing your
entire family.

From an early age Jesus
knew his birthday parties would
be well attended...

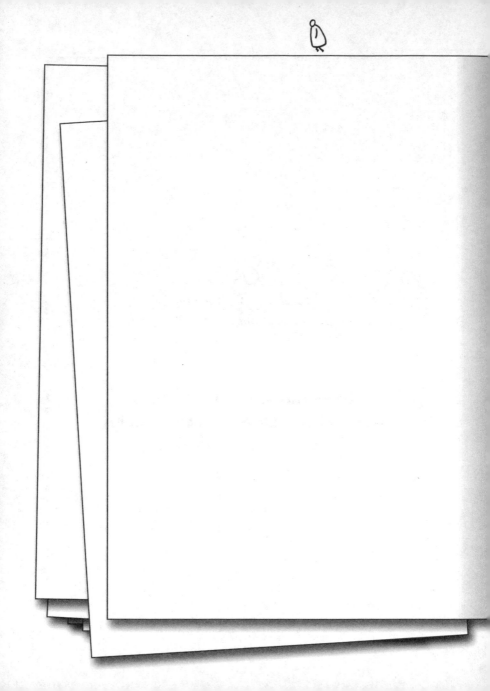

...due to the
water to wine ratio.

There are two reasons
why loving you is easy.
Number one: you're beautiful...

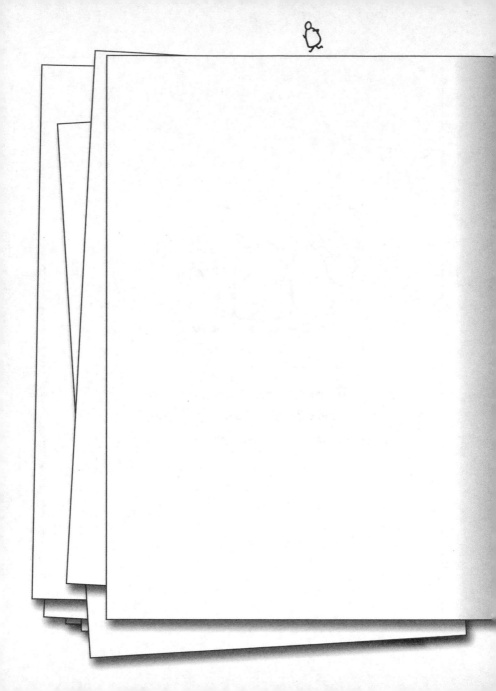

Number two:
I'm really shallow.

Failing to graduate closes
a few employment doors...

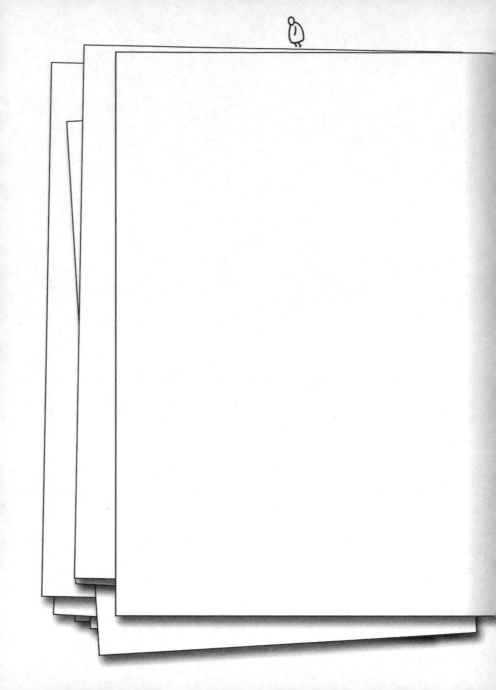

...but opens a few others.

Santa's recruitment policies
were tough...

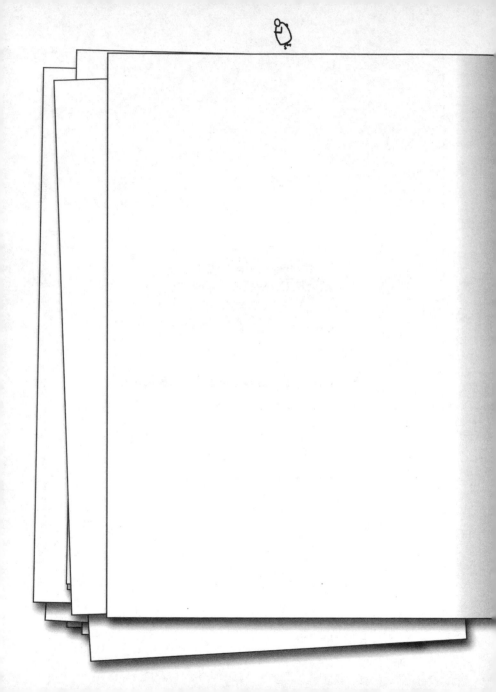

...but racist.

God loves a trier...

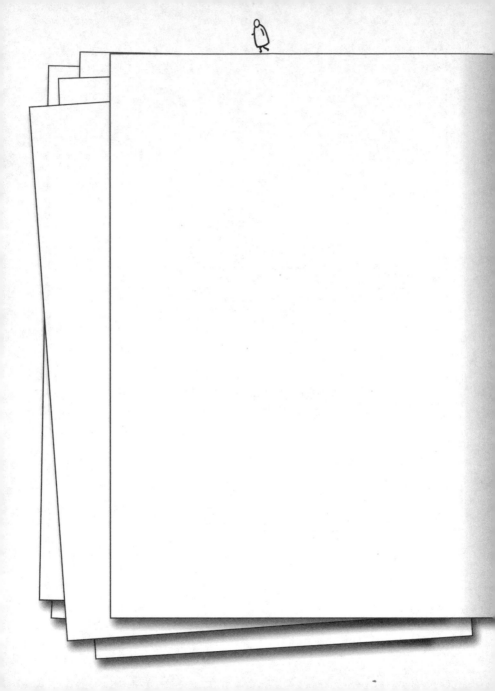

But it kind of pisses him off
when people don't live up
to their potential.

You should have had a ball
on your holidays...

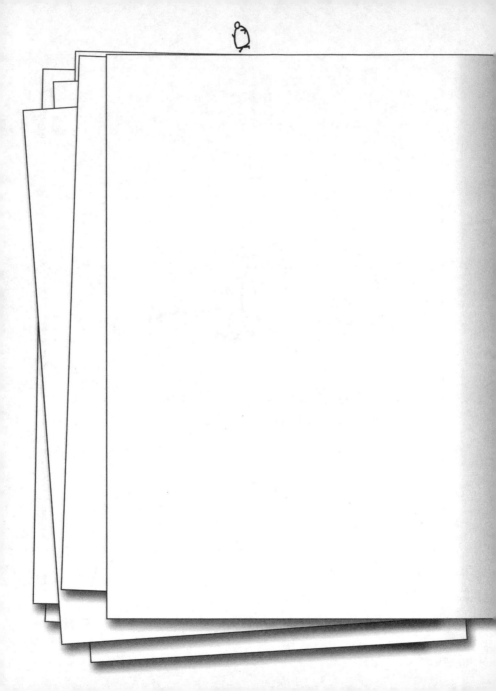

You shouldn't have let me look
after your dog.

Everybody loves
a happy ending...

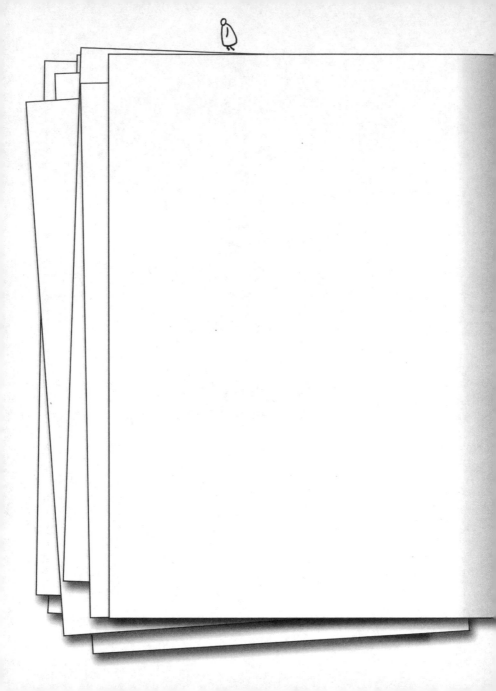

...except me. It's over.

I never said it was unusual
to go out at any time...

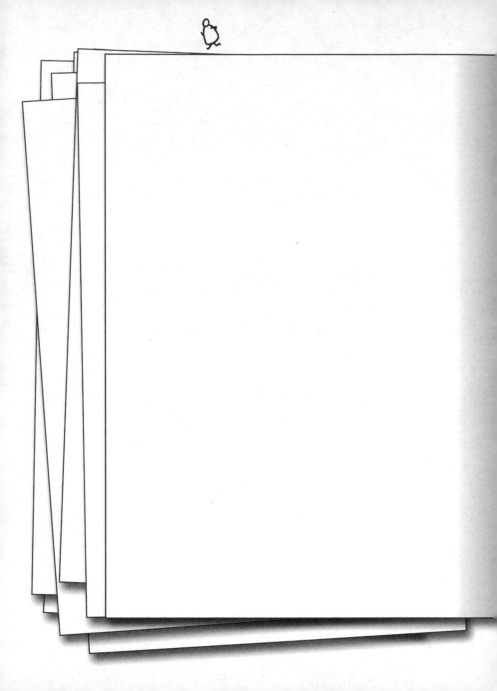

...but it is unusual to sleep with someone each time you do.

This Christmas spare a thought
for those less fortunate than you.

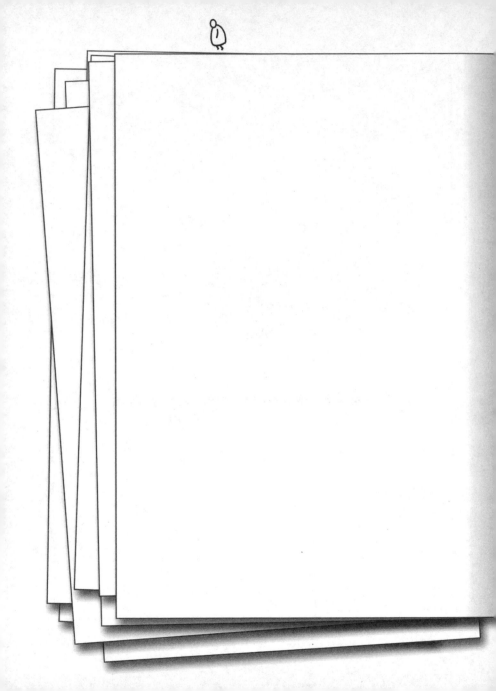

But don't let it ruin your day.

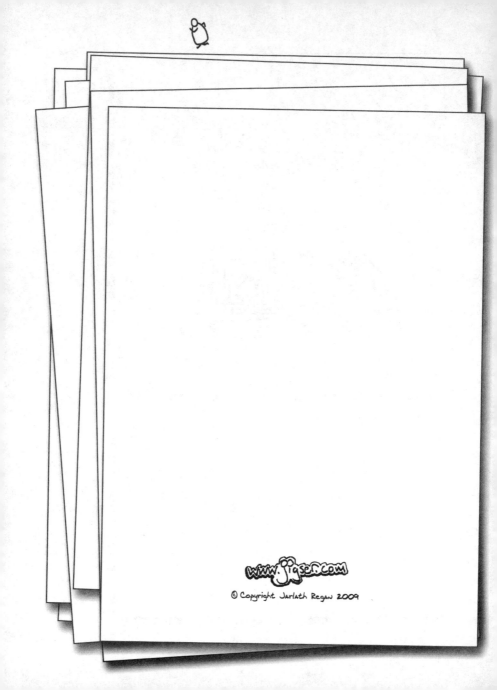

We've shared so many happy
memories and enjoyed some
wonderful times together.
I want you to know...

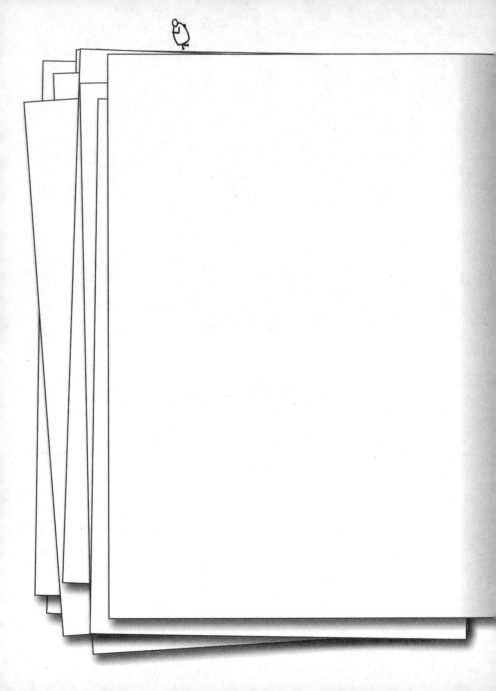

...that I am a robot and
as such incapable of love.

Attack is the best
form of defence...

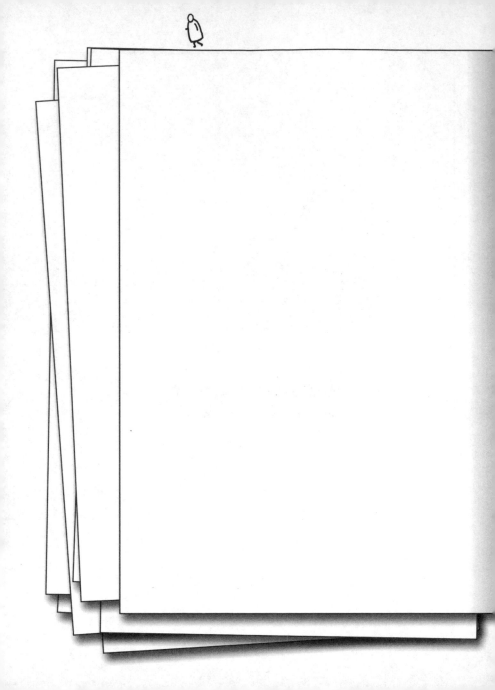

Except in a court of law.

It's the journey not the
destination that matters...

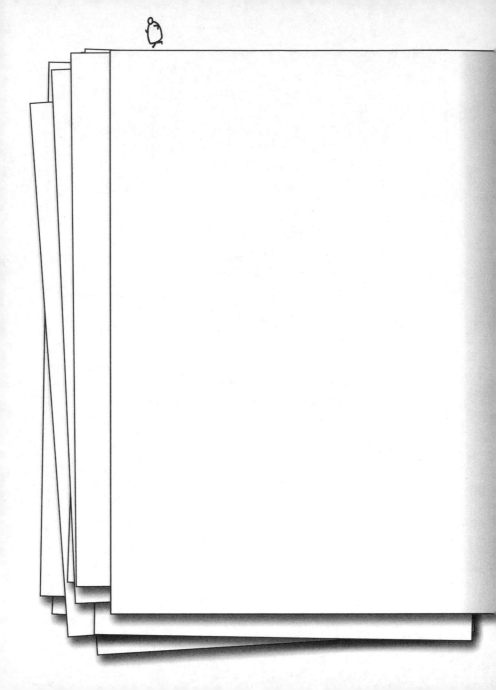

Unless you're going
to Disneyland!

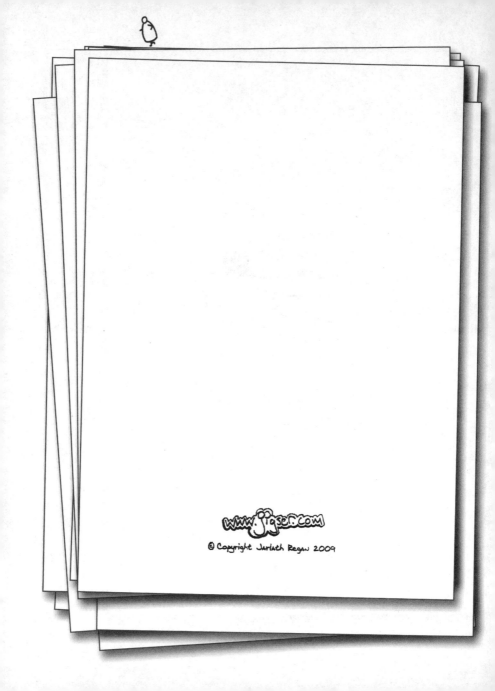

We've become so close...

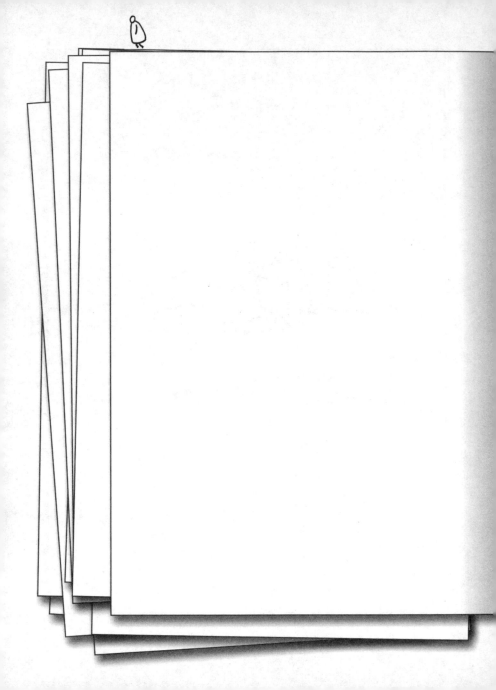

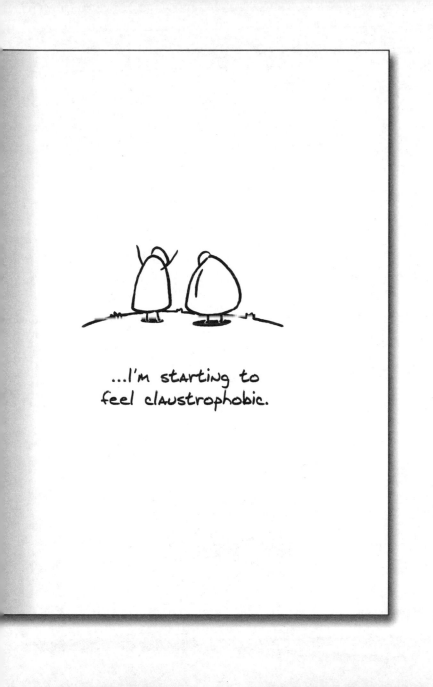

...I'm starting to
feel claustrophobic.

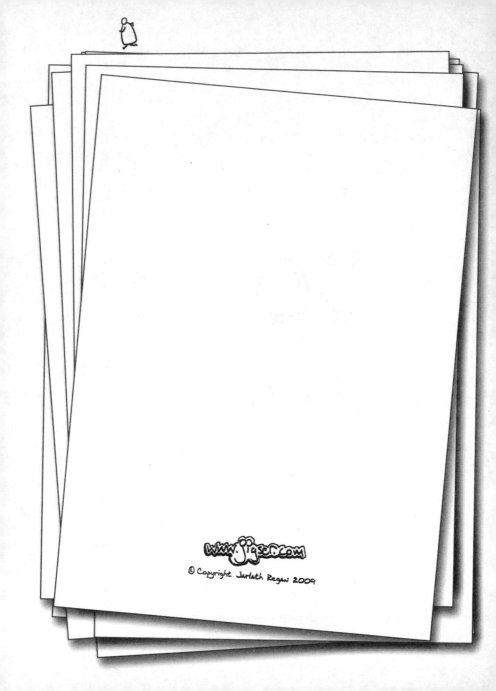

If you're dreaming of a white
Christmas you're like me...

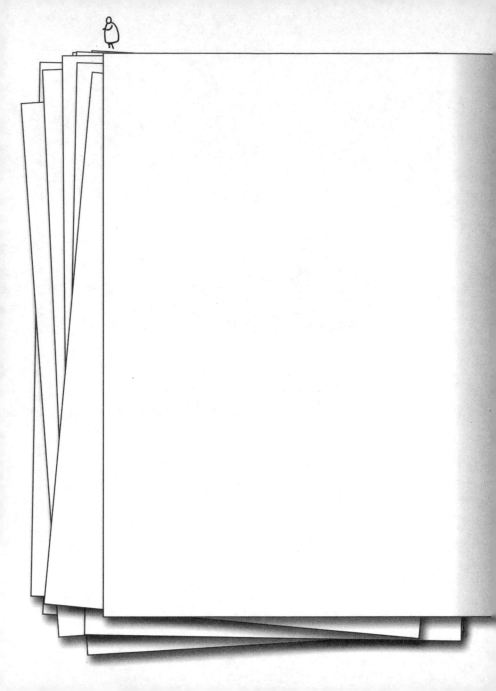

A racist.

The truth is St Patrick
didn't kill ALL the
snakes in Ireland...

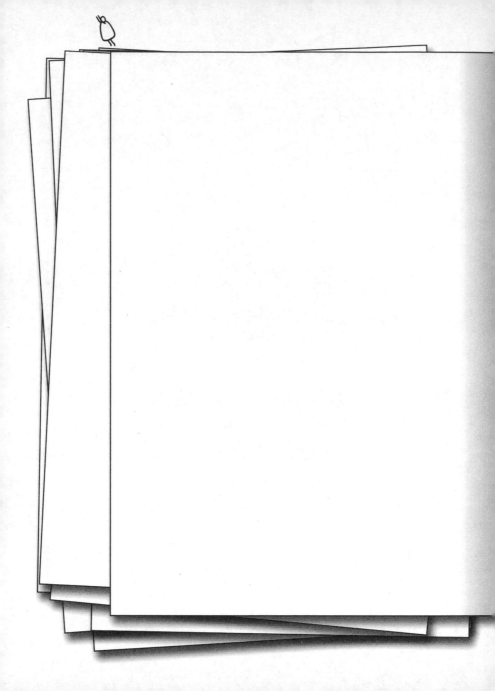

He killed the only
snake in Ireland.
The guy who owned it
was seriously pissed off about
it for ages.

Kids always make me smile...

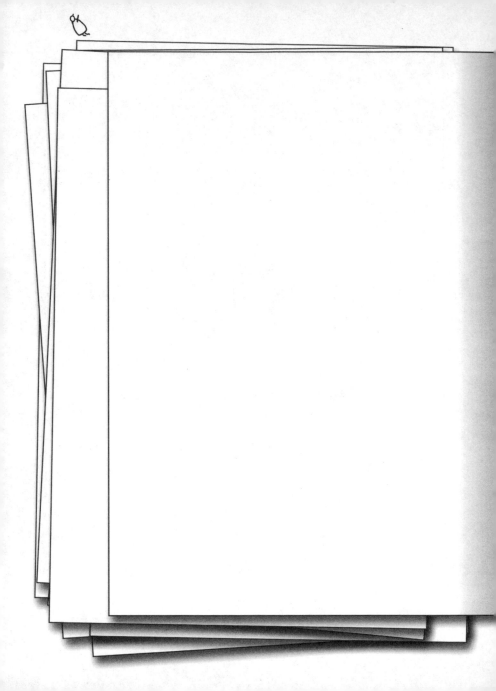

...and feel thankful
that I don't have any.

I heard you were complaining
about feeling sick
so I got you these pills...

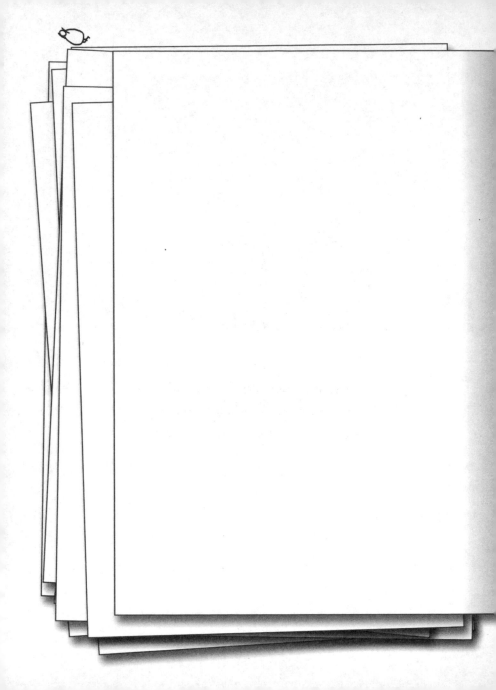

They're called
extra-strength 'Shut
the Fuck Up' tablets.

Make this Christmas Day
one they'll remember for ever...

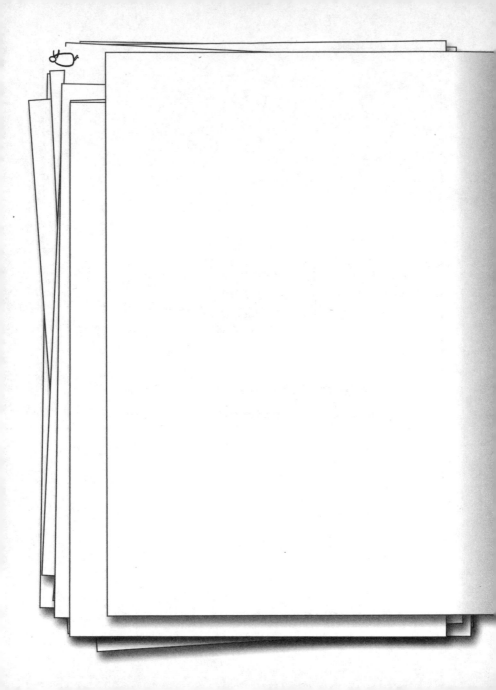

Thanks to his unique
genetic make-up, the Easter
Bunny rarely needs sleep,
smells of flowers and...

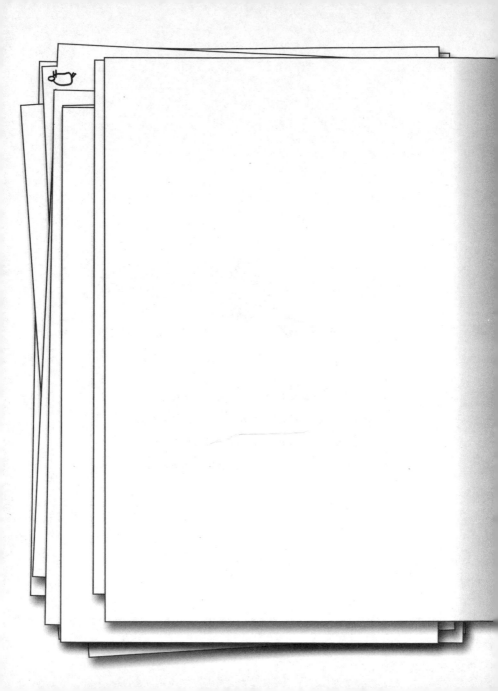

...shits chocolate.

I've been dying to see you
so I could tell you in person...

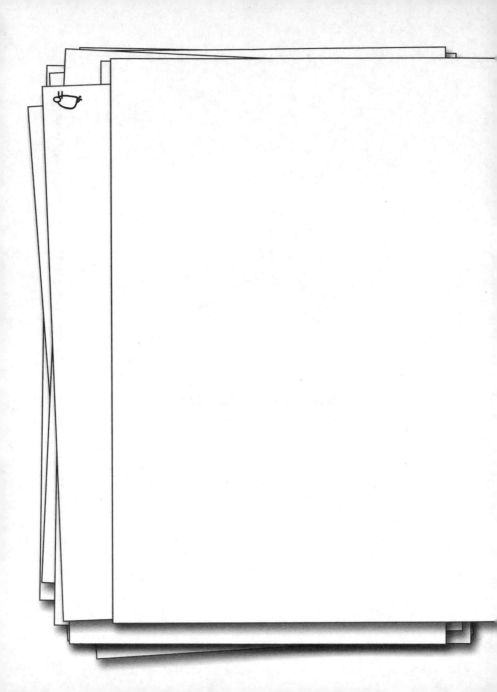

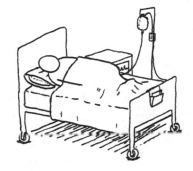

I'm dying.

Child abduction is
never funny...

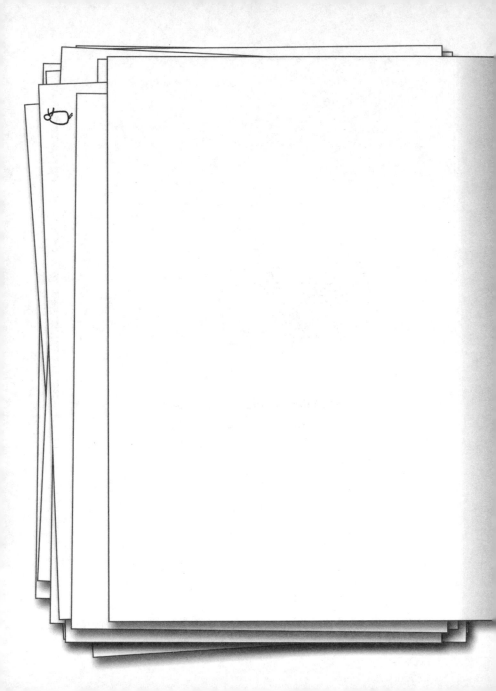

Except when it's a practical joke!
Your child can be found at:

(Address): _____

_____

_____

_____

A gift is a good expression
of a person's love for you...

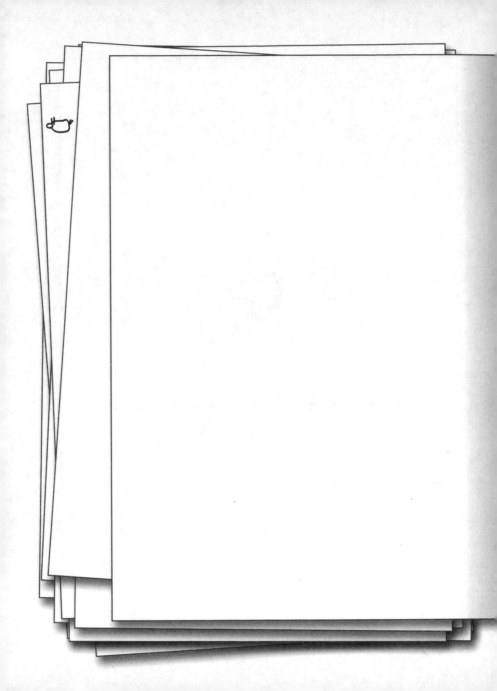

And a great source of
leverage in a future argument.

Behind Rudolph's shiny
red nose lay a dark secret
that only he knew.

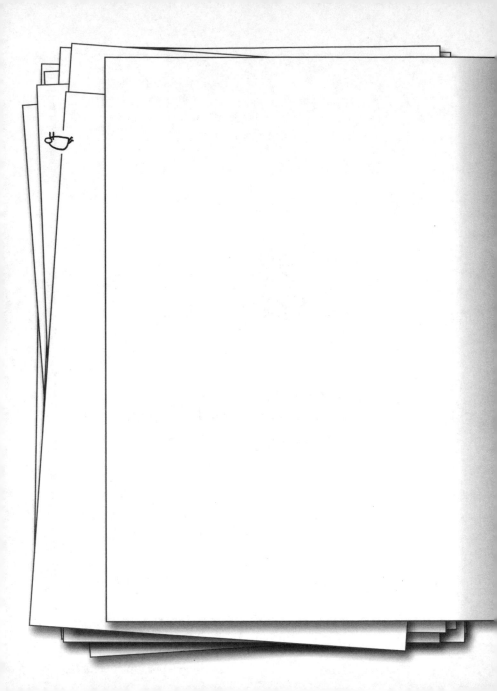

Will you marry me?

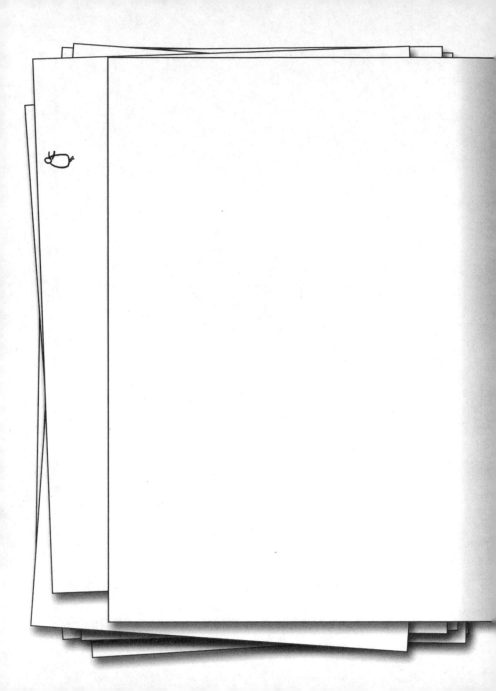

Only messin', I think
we should see other people.

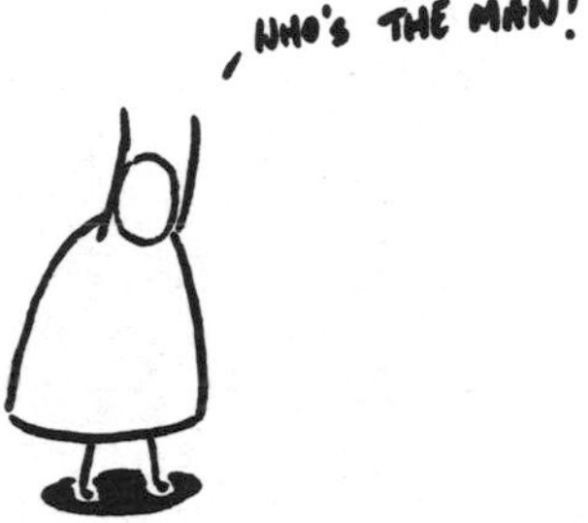

Congratulations
on being so deadly!

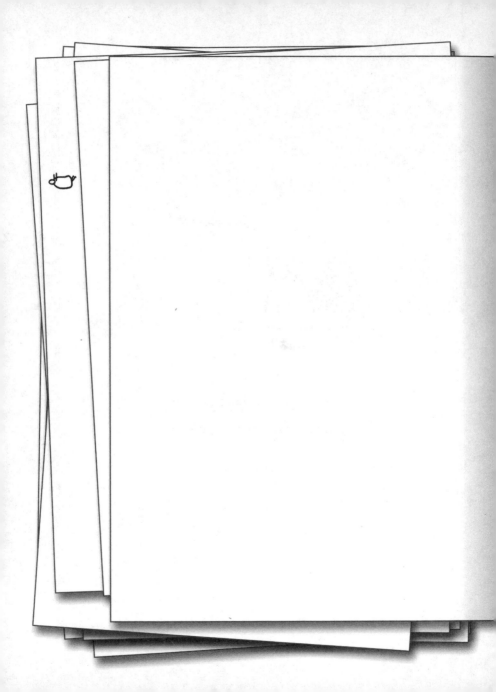

Make sure you don't
disappear up your own hole.

My love for you goes on
and on and on and on and on...

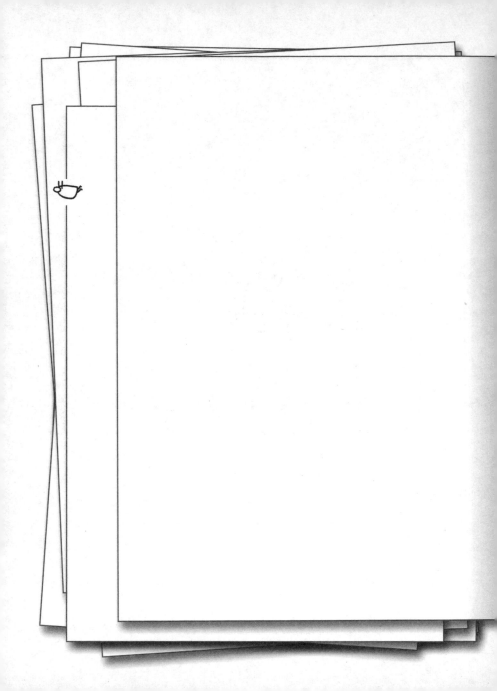

A bit like one of
your stories.

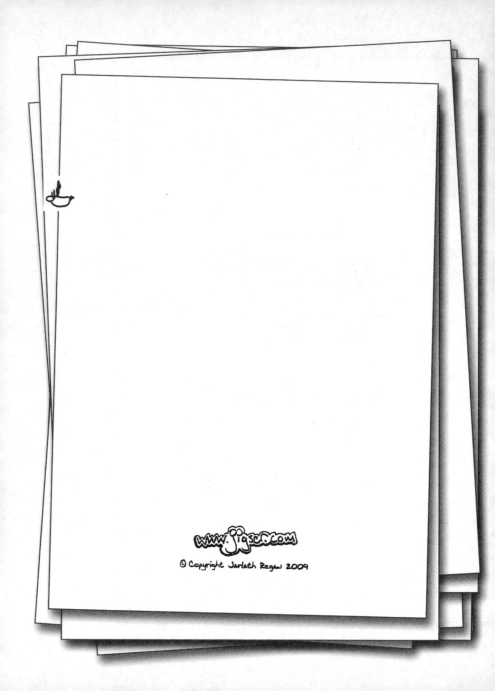

You know you're getting old
when people look confused
and ask you what the hell
you're talking about...

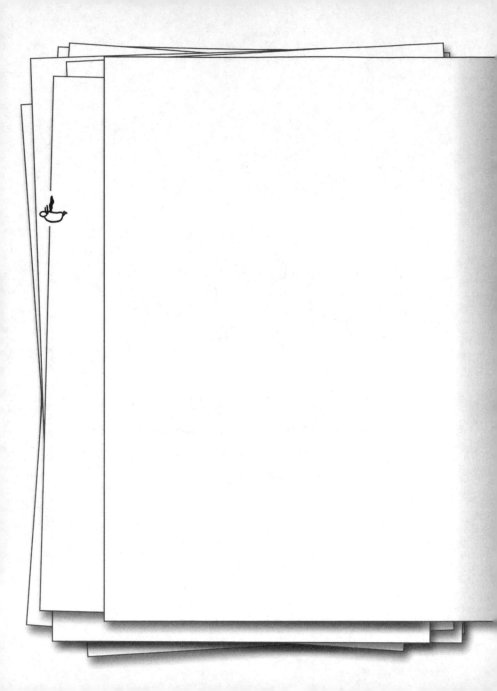

And you didn't even
realize you were talking.

www.jigser.com

© Copyright Jarlath Regan 2009

Last night I saw my
mother kissing Santa Claus...

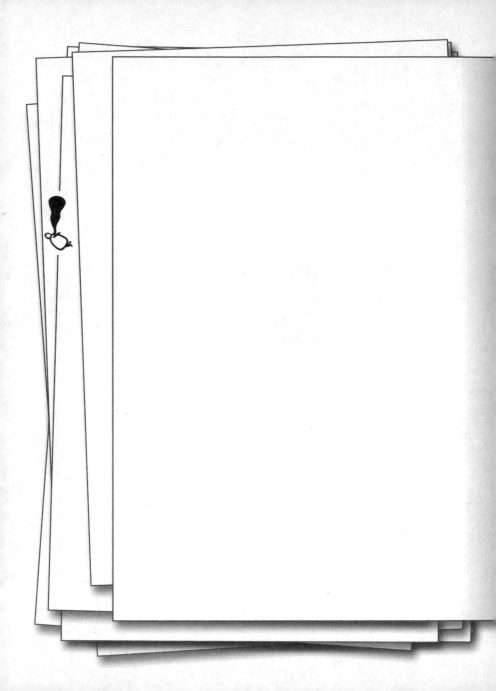

And then he appeared
to pee in her mouth.

You have to admit,
we have a lot in common.
You like the Beatles, I like
the Beatles; I have a large
knife collection...

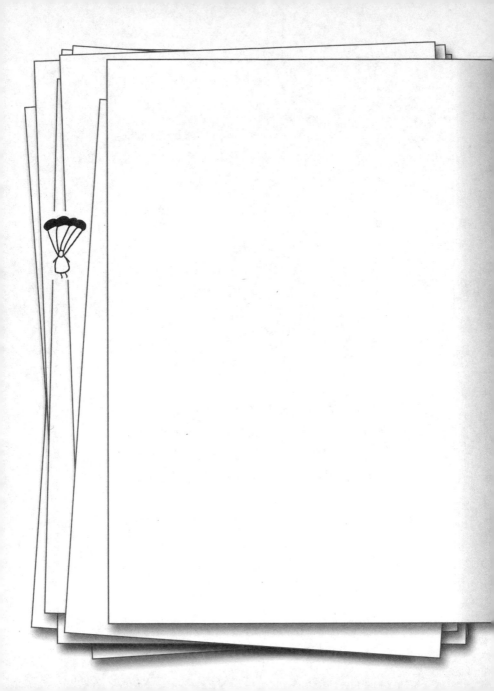

You're gonna die.

The biggest thing we have
to fear is fear itself...

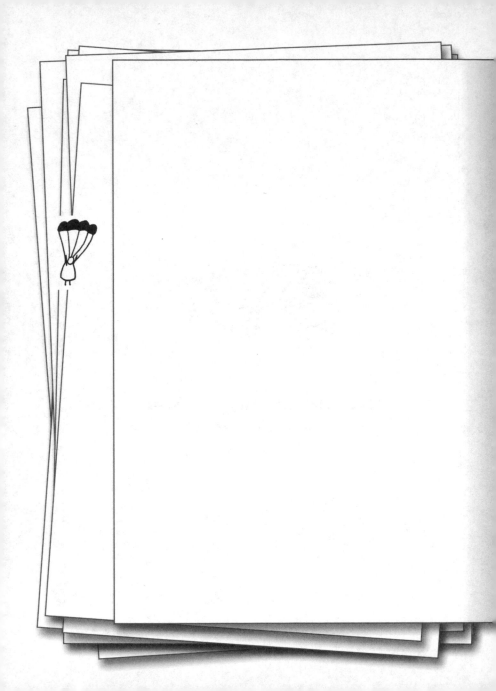

...and bears.

If music is the food of love...

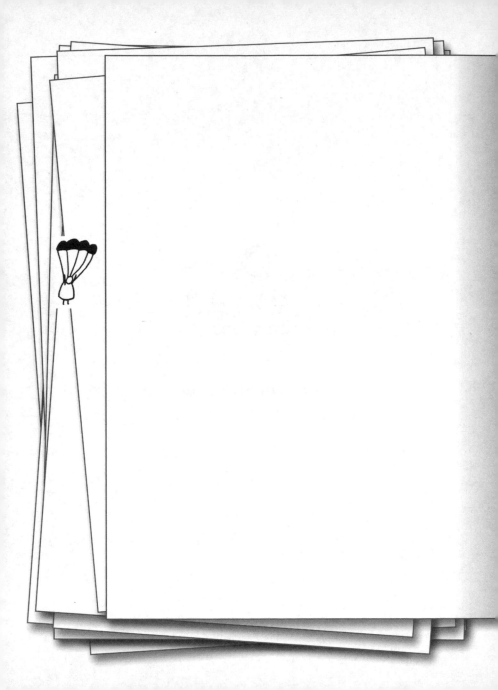

Your dancing is the diarrhoea.

www.jigser.com

© Copyright Jarlath Regan 2009

I know we've had our
differences in the past, so
I want you to know...

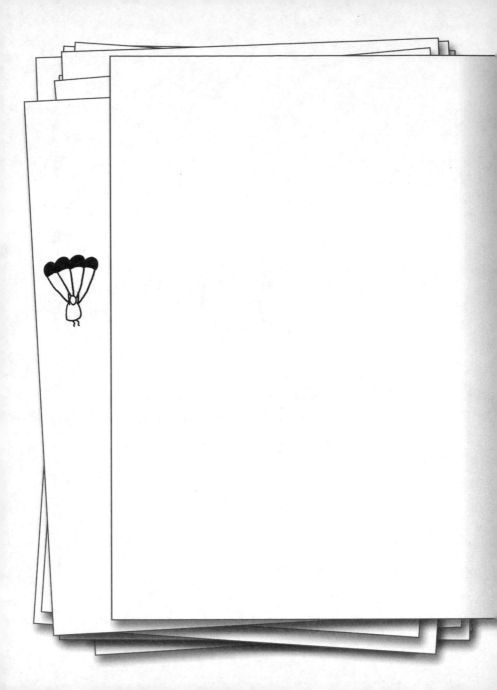

Most people I know
think that I'm sound
and that you're an arsehole.

The elves knew that Christmas
was a stressful time...

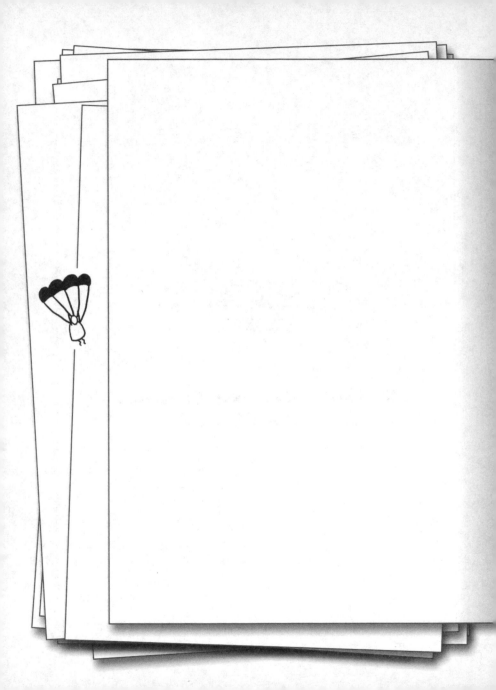

But Santa's behaviour
this year was inexcusable.

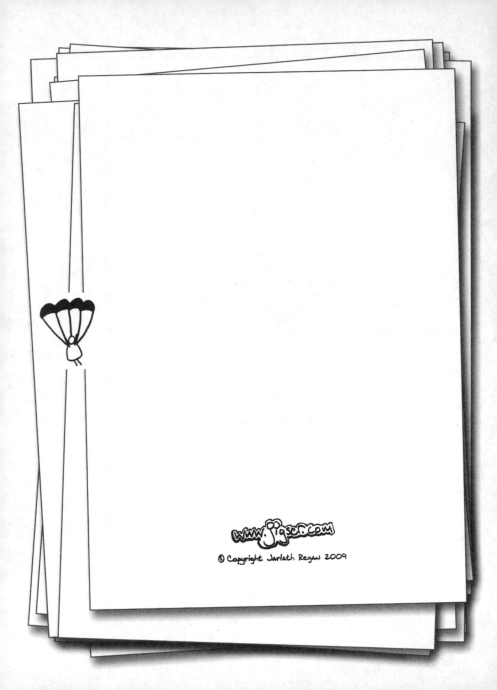

I love every single
little bit of you...

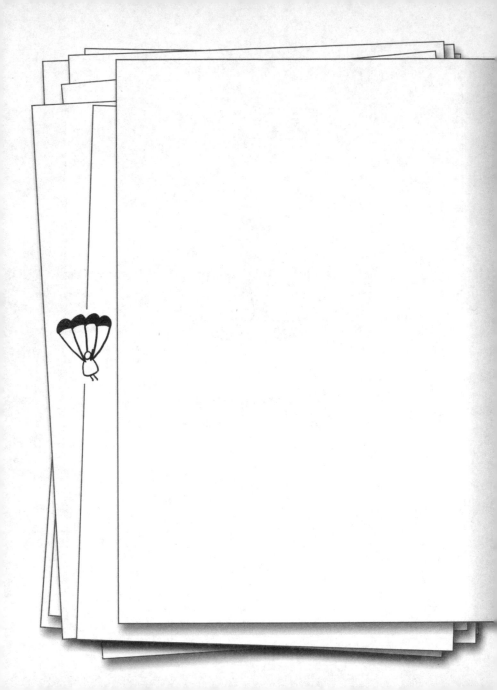

Even your tiny dick.

Things can only get better...

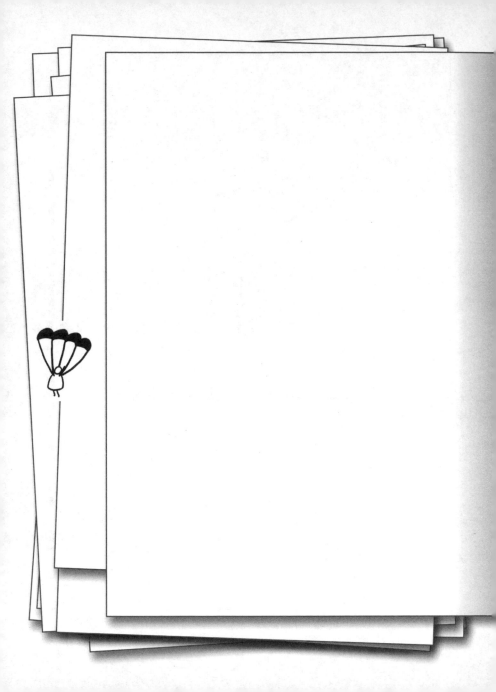

but that's not a guarantee.

www.jigser.com

© Copyright Jarlath Regan 2009

When you're a child,
Christmas is a magical time.
Then your parents tell you...

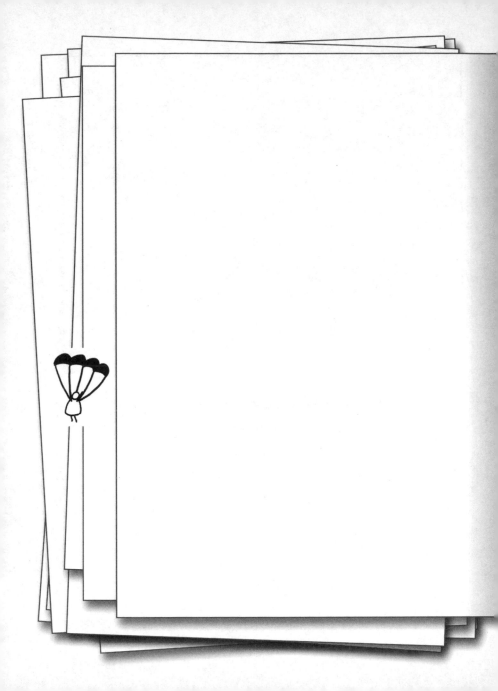

...there's no such
thing as Jesus.

In love, it's the little things
that make all the difference.
I guess what I'm trying to say is...

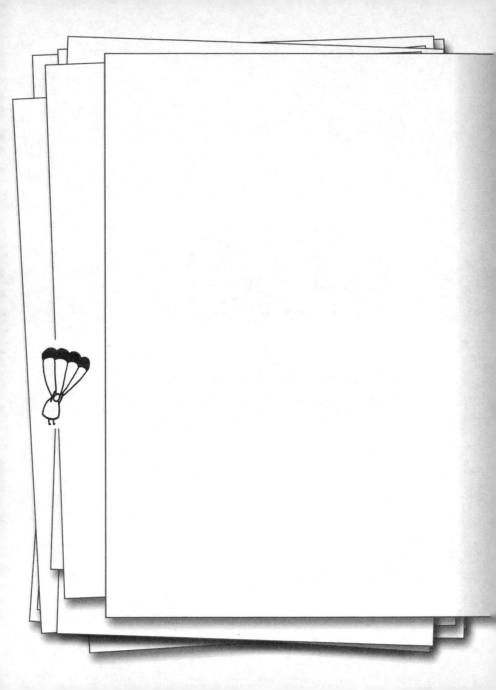

I love your tits.

AND THEN IT BLEW UP!

Kids say the
darndest things...

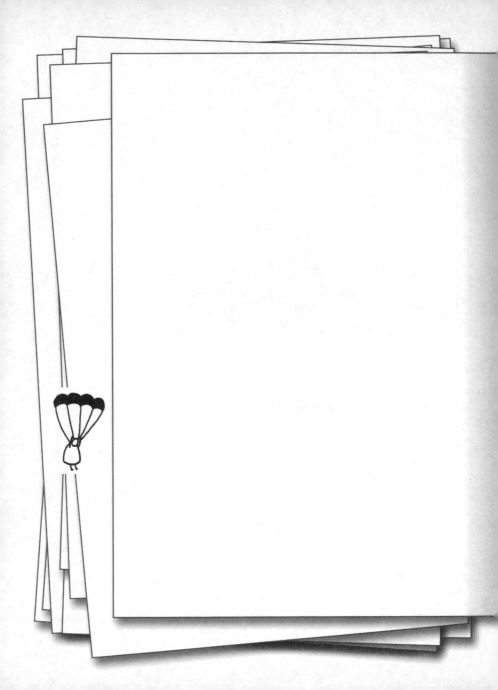

But if your kid says
that I touched him,
he's a fucking liar.

Happy Valentine's Day.
I will always love you
but if you don't love me...

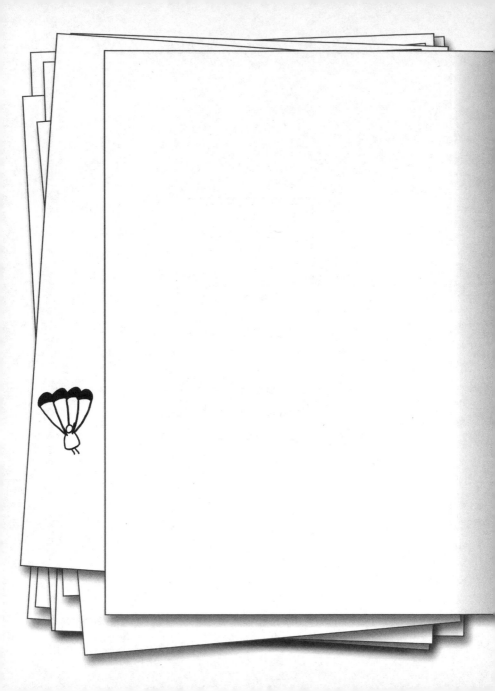

I'll do it myself.

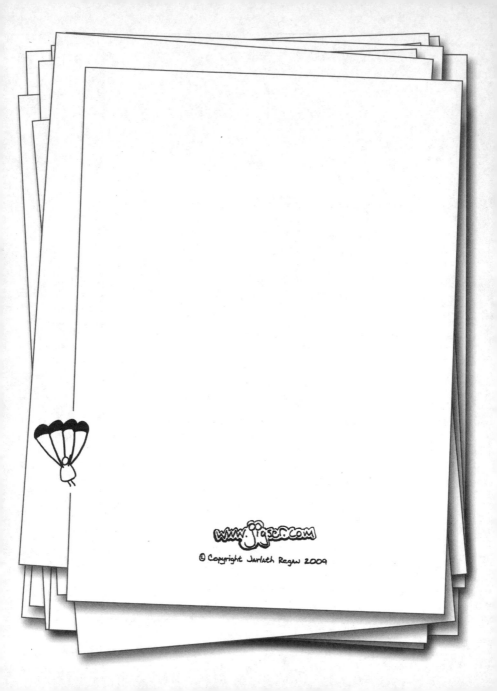

Why do people say, 'It'll be Christmas before you know it'?

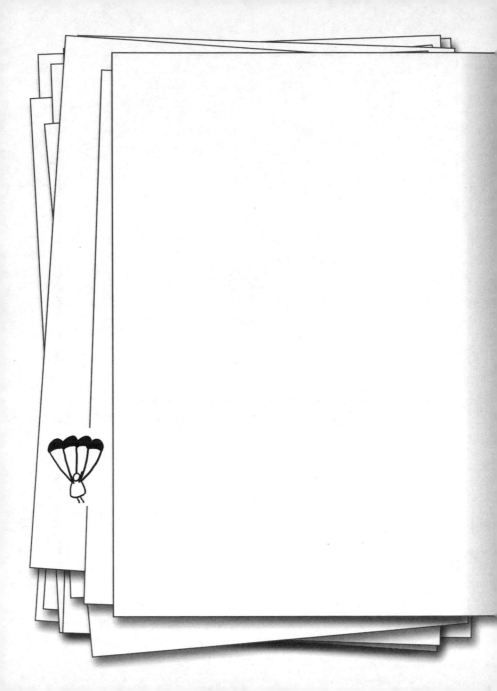

That's never happened
to anyone. Ever.

www.jigser.com

© Copyright Jarlath Regan 2009

Will you kiss me
under the mistletoe?

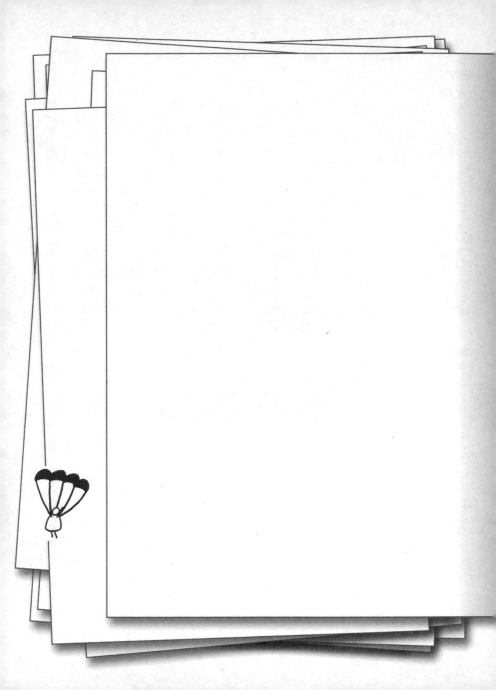

Are you kidding me? I wouldn't
kiss you under anaesthetic.

'Tis better to have tried
and failed than never
to have tried at all...

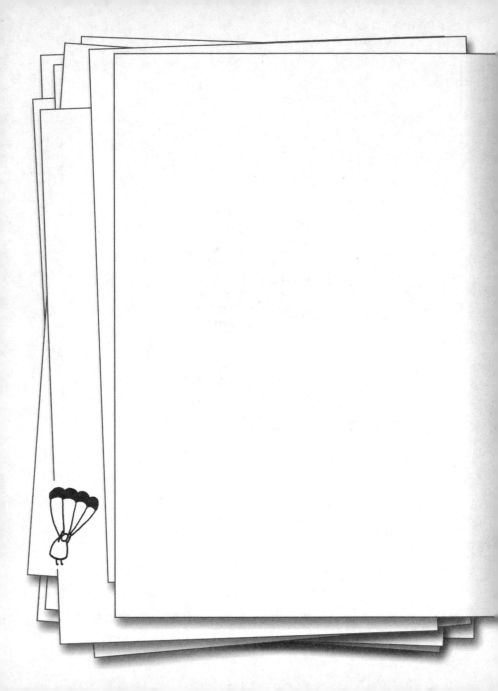

Unless you make a
real tit out of yourself.

Don't forget the true
reason for Christmas...

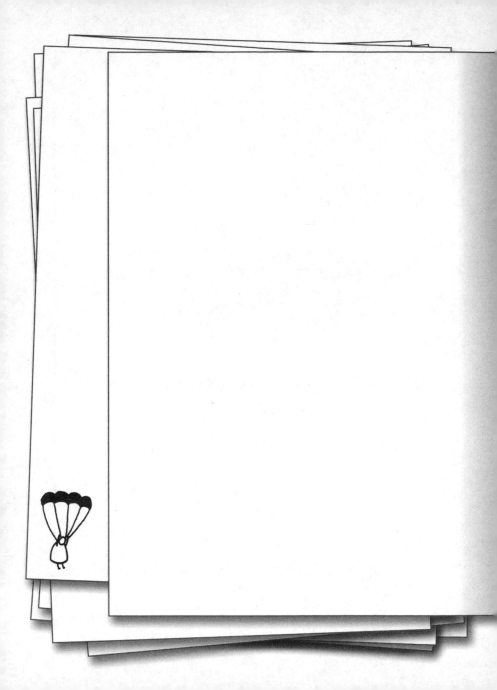

Santa Claus
died for our sins.

Your eyes remind me of Paris
in the springtime...

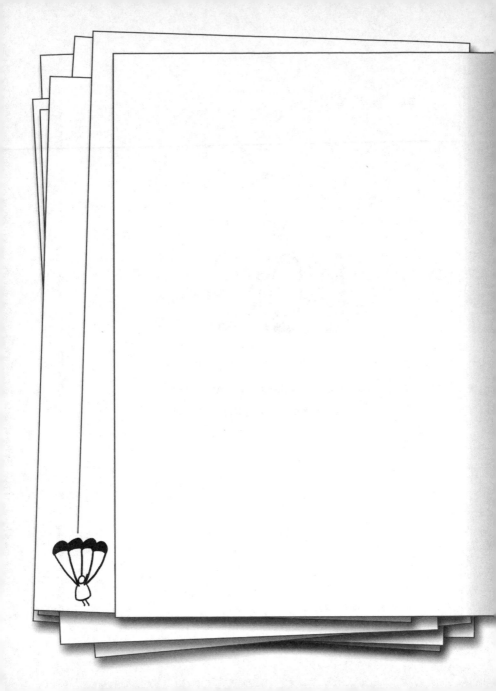

It's a pity your breath
reminds me of
the Metro in summer.

www.jigser.com

© Copyright Jarlath Regan 2009

How would you feel
about having a baby?

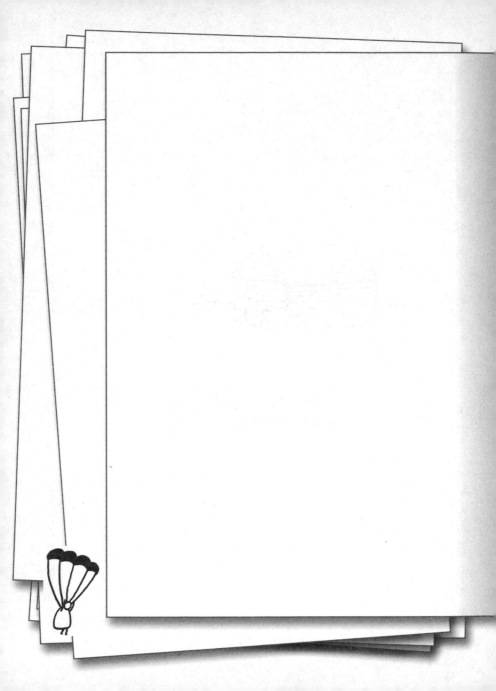

Good.
I left it in the shed.

The elves worked diligently
because they loved children
and toys but most of all...

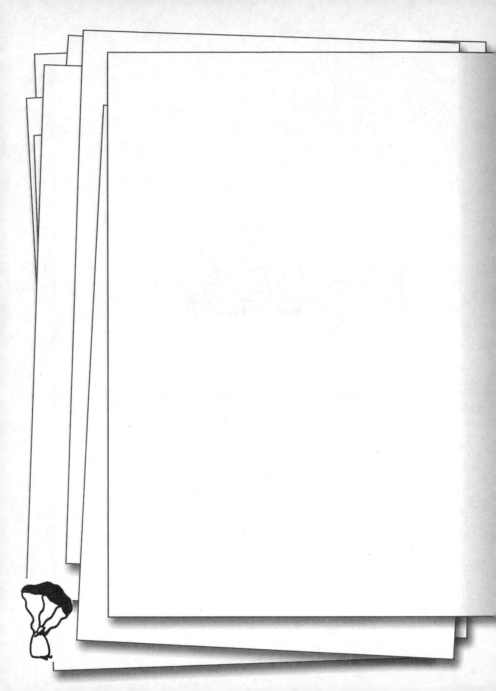

...they feared Santa
and his fits of rage.

Santa brings toys to all
the good boys and girls...

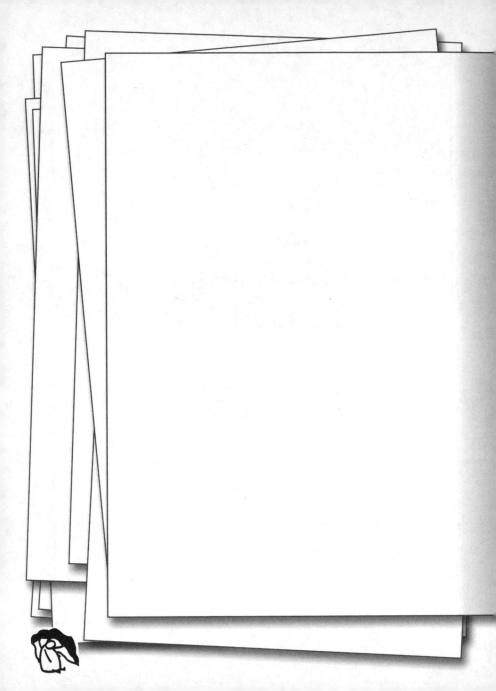

As well as some of the
more entertaining bold ones.

You're in my heart,
you're in my dreams,
you're in my future...

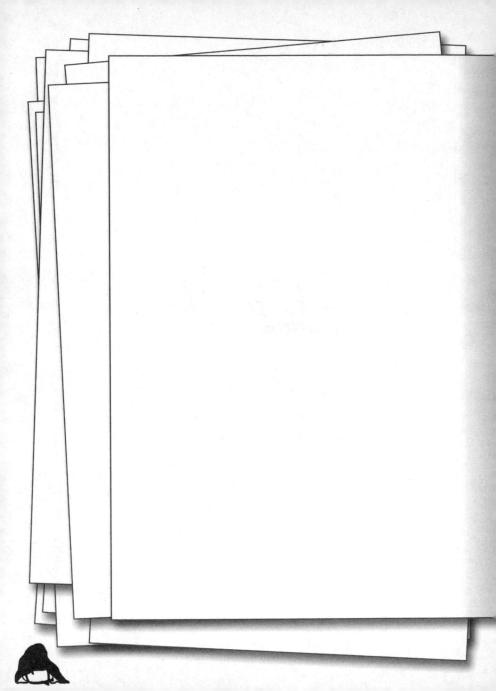

Please stay out of
my private shit.

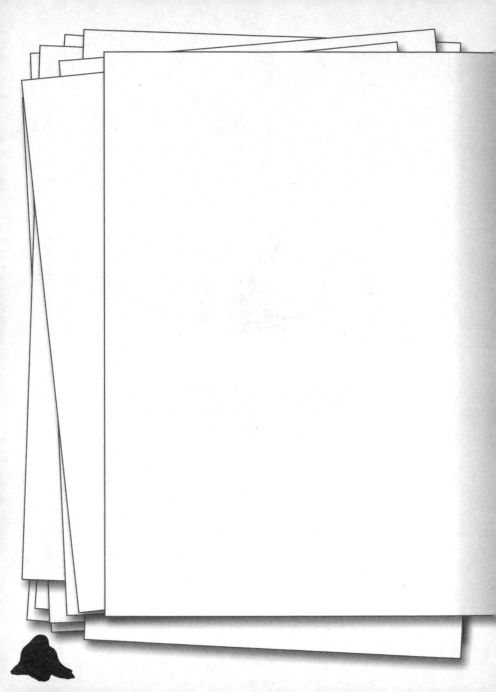